A Fun Winter Day

BY JENNA LEE GLEISNER

The Child's World®
childsworld.com

Published by The Child's World®
1980 Lookout Drive • Mankato, MN 56003-1705
800-599-READ • www.childsworld.com

Photographs ©: iStockphoto, cover, 1, 5, 6–7, 9, 17;
Xi Xin Xing/iStockphoto, 10–11; Dmitry Trubitsyn/
Shutterstock Images, 13; Shutterstock Images, 14;
Antonio Diaz/iStockphoto, 18–19; Yuganov Konstantin/
Shutterstock Images, 20; Red Line Editorial, 22

ISBN 9781503823846
LCCN 2017945002

Printed in the United States of America
PA02359

ABOUT THE AUTHOR

Jenna Lee Gleisner is an author
and editor who lives in Minnesota.
She has written more than 80
books for children. When not
writing or editing, she enjoys
spending time with her family
and her dog, Norrie.

Contents

Snow Day

It snowed last night.

Today is a **snow day**!

People put on coats and boots. They wear mittens and hats.

Fun in the Snow

Kids play in the snow.

They make **snow angels**.

Families build snowmen.
They put hats and
scarves on the snowmen.

Some kids build snow **forts**. Who can make the biggest fort?

Some people go sledding.
They zoom down hills
on sleds.

Warming Up

Later, people warm up.

They drink hot chocolate.

Warm treats taste good on cold days. Some people **bake** cookies.

18

Some people make **crafts**.
It has been a fun
winter day!

Marshmallow Snowman

Make a snowman you can eat!

Supplies:

1 graham cracker
2 marshmallows
4 mini chocolate chips
1 candy corn

2 pretzel sticks
knife
frosting

Instructions:

1. Spread frosting on the graham cracker. Stick one marshmallow on top.

2. Frost the top of the marshmallow and stick another on top.

3. Insert two chocolate chips for buttons and another two for eyes.

4. Poke a candy corn in the top marshmallow as the nose. Poke the pretzels into the sides as arms.

Glossary

bake—(BAYK) To bake is to cook food in an oven with dry heat. Some people bake warm foods on cold winter days.

crafts—(KRAFTZ) Crafts are objects that are made to be useful, fun, or beautiful. A fun indoor winter activity is making crafts.

forts—(FORTS) Forts are buildings that protect people. Some kids build snow forts on a snow day.

snow angels—(SNOH AYN-juhlz) Snow angels are designs made in fresh snow by lying on your back and moving your arms and legs up and down. Kids make snow angels in winter.

snow day—(SNOH DAY) A snow day is a day on which school is closed due to heavy snowfall. Kids play in the snow on a snow day.

To Learn More

Books

Appleby, Alex. *It's Snowing!*
New York, NY: Gareth Stevens
Publishing, 2014.

Lindeen, Mary. *Winter*. Chicago, IL:
Norwood House Press, 2015.

Web Sites

Visit our Web site for links about
fun winter activities:
childsworld.com/links

*Note to Parents, Teachers, and Librarians: We routinely verify
our Web links to make sure they are safe and active sites. So
encourage your readers to check them out!*

Index